Life in the Temperate Forests

Life in the Temperate Forests

Salvatore Tocci

Franklin Watts
A Division of Scholastic Inc.
New York • Toronto • London • Auckland • Sydney
Mexico City • New Delhi • Hong Kong
Danbury, Connecticut

For Erik, with whom I plan to hike many trails in temperate forests

Note to readers: Definitions for words in **bold** can be found in the Glossary at the back of this book.

Photographs © 2005: Alamy Images: 5 top, 28 (Dynamic Graphics Group/Creatas), cover (David Lyons), 10, 11 (Robert Harding Picture Library Ltd.), 41 (Sarkis Images), 5 bottom, 48 (Stock Connection); Alaska Stock Images/Patrick Endres: 18, 19; Corbis Images: 17, 53 (Raymond Gehman), 26 bottom (Eric and David Hosking), 8, 9 (Robert Kaufman/Yogi, Inc.), 6 (David Muench), 32 (Pat O'Hara), 17 (Charles O'Rear), 54 (Owaki-Kulla), 34 (Michael Rose/Frank Lane Picture Agency), 2 (Royalty Free); Minden Pictures/Mark Moffett: 31; Peter Arnold Inc.: 46 (S. J. Krasemann), 52 (Ed Reschke); Photo Researchers, NY: 45 (Scott Camazine), 22 (Jeff Greenberg), 38 (Tom and Pat Leeson), 1 (Jeff Lepore), 24 (Robert Noonan); photolibrary.com: 21 (Irvine Cushing/OSF), 30 (Rob Nunnington/OSF); The Image Bank/Getty Images/Joseph Van Os: 15; Visuals Unlimited/Jack Bostrack: 26 top.

Illustrations by: Bob Italiano

The photograph on the cover shows the Great Smoky Mountains in the Appalachian range in North Carolina. The photograph opposite the title page shows a temperate forest in the northwestern United States.

Library of Congress Cataloging-in-Publication Data

Tocci, Salvatore.
  Life in the temperate forests / Salvatore Tocci.— 1st ed.
    p. cm. — (Watts library)
  Includes bibliographical references and index.
  ISBN 0-531-12363-4
  1. Forest ecology—Juvenile literature. I. Title. II. Series.
  QH84.3.T63 2005
  577.3—dc22   2004027303

Contents

Introduction
A Very Long Hike 7

Chapter One
The World's Temperate Forests 11

Chapter Two
Threats to the Forests 19

Chapter Three
Plants of the Forest 29

Chapter Four
Animals of the Forest 39

Chapter Five
Forest Fires 49

55 **Glossary**

58 **To Find Out More**

60 **A Note on Sources**

61 **Index**

The Appalachian Trail is the longest footpath in the world, stretching across fourteen states.

A Very Long Hike

In 1948, Earl Shaffer became the first person to hike all 2,168 miles (3,488 kilometers) of the Appalachian Trail in a single journey. At the time, most people thought that anyone trying to hike the entire trail had to do it in stages. Perhaps a person could hike the trail for several days, rest for a few days, and then return to continue the journey. Hiking the entire Appalachian Trail in one trip seemed impossible.

Mount Katahdin is the northern starting point of the Appalachian Trail.

It took Shaffer four months, but he did it. He hiked all the way from Springer Mountain in Georgia to Mount Katahdin in Maine. Shaffer became what is known as the first through-hiker of the Appalachian Trail.

In 1965, Shaffer through-hiked the entire trail again, this time walking from Maine to Georgia. He became the first person to complete through-hikes in both directions.

The Youngest

A six-year-old boy became the young-est through-hiker when he walked the Appalachian Trail in 1980 with his parents.

Then, in 1998, Shaffer completed his third through-hike. Just two weeks shy of his eightieth birthday, he became the oldest person to through-hike the trail. Shaffer is one of few people to have spent a great deal of time hiking through the **temperate forest**—a type of forest that is only found in certain parts of the world.

Part of the Appalachian Trail passes through Shenandoah National Park in Virginia.

Chapter One

The World's Temperate Forests

Scientists divide Earth into different ecological areas called **biomes.** A biome is an area where environmental conditions determine the types of plants and animals that can live there. These environmental conditions include how much sunlight and precipitation an area receives.

The Appalachian Trail passes through a biome known as the temperate forest.

The word *forest* indicates that trees are plentiful in this biome. The word *temperate* means that the climate gets neither too hot, as it does in the tropics, nor too cold, as it does near the poles.

Earth's Temperate Zones

Places where the summers do not get too hot and the winters do not get too cold are found in Earth's temperate zones. There are two temperate zones. One temperate zone is in the **Northern Hemisphere.** This zone extends from the Tropic of Cancer to the Arctic Circle. In North America, the temperate zone stretches from central Mexico to northern Canada.

The other temperate zone is in the **Southern Hemisphere.** This zone extends from the Tropic of Capricorn to the Antarctic Circle. Using South America as a reference point, it stretches from northern Argentina to the coast of Antarctica.

As its name suggests, a temperate forest grows only in a temperate zone. Temperate forests, though, are primarily in

The Five with Names

Latitude lines circle maps of Earth in an east-west direction. They are recorded on charts and maps as numbers and help people navigate. Only five lines of latitude have names. Going from north to south, these circles are called the Arctic Circle, the Tropic of Cancer, the equator, the Tropic of Capricorn, and the Antarctic Circle.

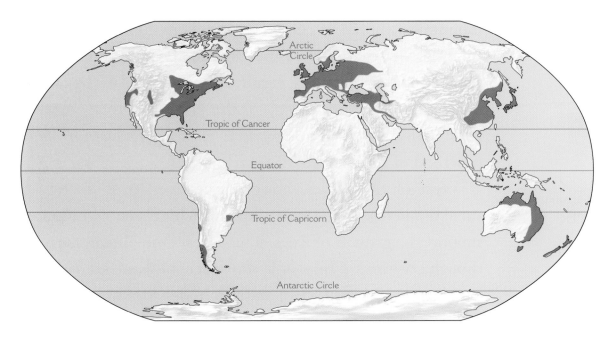

the temperate zone of the Northern Hemisphere for the simple reason that most of the temperate zone in the Southern Hemisphere is covered by ocean. Even where there is land in the southern temperate zone, however, the climate does not always favor the growth of a temperate forest.

Which parts of the world have the most temperate forests?

The Southern Temperate Zone

Parts of South America, including most of Argentina and all of Uruguay, lie within the southern temperate zone. Yet neither country has a temperate forest. The Andes Mountains, which run along the western border of Argentina, are the reason. Winds usually blow from west to east in this part of the world. Any wind carrying moisture from the Pacific Ocean must first pass over the Andes Mountains before it reaches Argentina and Uruguay. As it crosses the mountains, the air is cooled and loses its moisture. By the time the air reaches the other side of the Andes, it has little, if any, moisture. As a result, Argentina and Uruguay do not get enough rain to support the growth of trees. A temperate forest needs to receive at least 12 inches (30 centimeters) of rain per year.

West of the Andes, however, the climate is wetter. A small temperate forest is in Chile, which gets enough rain to support the growth of trees. This forest is small and narrow, though, because Chile is a thin slice of land sandwiched between the Pacific Ocean and the Andes Mountains.

The only other places with temperate forests in the southern temperate zone are southeastern Australia, Tasmania, and New Zealand. The islands of Tasmania and New Zealand can get more than 40 inches (102 cm) of rain each year. These islands are covered with lush temperate forests. In Australia, a temperate forest grows only in the southeast. This part of the country receives enough rain to support the trees because of the moisture coming in from the Pacific Ocean.

The Northern Temperate Zone

Temperate forests once covered almost the entire eastern United States, as well as parts of southeastern Canada. Today, these forests make up only a small part of the landscape. Many of the trees have been cleared to make way for farms, villages, towns, and cities.

A Dry Land

A desert, which is another type of biome, may receive less than 0.5 inch (1.3 cm) of rain per year.

The temperate forest of New Zealand and Tasmania resembles a tropical rain forest, which is a biome in warmer and much wetter climates near the equator.

Texas-Size

All the temperate forests in Tasmania, New Zealand, and Australia combined occupy an area about the size of Texas.

15

Temperate forests are also in eastern Asia, including parts of Japan, Korea, and China. Japan is made up of some three thousand islands. Many of these islands were formed in the last few thousand years by volcanoes rising from the ocean floor. Today, rugged mountains cover much of these islands, and temperate forests grow in many of the valleys.

The climate in Korea is ideal for supporting the growth of temperate forests. As a result, they cover much of Korea. Korea's temperate forests span an area about the size of Ohio.

China is a very large country, with a land area about the same as that of the United States. Its temperate forests, however, cover an area less than half the size of Alaska, the largest

In Portugal and Spain, the bark is stripped from oak trees to make corks for wine bottles.

of the fifty states. At one time, the temperate forests of China covered a much larger area, perhaps stretching across China, into Russia, and as far as Eastern Europe.

The temperate forests in Europe also once covered a much larger area. Today, many of the European forests are gone because the trees were cleared to make way for farms and homes. The forests that remain are scattered across Europe, from Portugal in the west to Russia in the east, and from Denmark in the north to Italy in the south.

The Bialowieza Forest, which is on the border between Poland and Belarus, is the largest surviving fragment of the temperate forests that once covered much of Europe. At one time, this forest belonged to the Polish royal family, which used it as a private hunting ground. Today, the Bialowieza Forest is protected by the United Nations, which has established areas that are off-limits to hunters.

The European bison in the Bialowieza Forest were one of the favorite targets of hunters. Today, more than five hundred bison roam the park since being reintroduced after the last wild bison was shot in 1919.

Massive ice sheets similar to this one once covered the land areas where temperate forests grow today.

Chapter Two

Threats to the Forests

Earth's climate has gone through several cycles of warm and cold periods that each lasted for millions of years. The cold periods are known as ice ages. During each ice age, huge glaciers advanced from the north and south poles to cover enormous regions of the planet, including much of the temperate zones. As the glaciers advanced over the land, they wiped out the temperate forests. In the United States, these forests survived by extending farther south.

The glaciers of the last ice age retreated about eleven thousand years ago. As the glaciers retreated, temperate forests reclaimed the land they once occupied. Much of the eastern United States again became home to a temperate forest.

Clearing the Forests

As the continental glaciers were retreating, prehistoric humans began to attach crude hand axes made of stone to the ends of long wooden handles. Now they no longer had to pound with their hands to use their stone tools. Instead, they could swing with their arms. Therefore, humans could use their axes to strike their targets with much greater force. One of their favorite targets became the trunks of the trees growing in the temperate forest.

At the time, the forests were not in danger of being wiped out. First, there were not many people chopping down trees. Second, these people cleared only small parcels of land or just enough to grow their crops. Third, these early farmers worked the land for several years and then moved on, which allowed the forest to grow back.

This pattern of clearing a small area of forest land, growing crops, and then moving on to more fertile land continued for thousands of years. This lifestyle gradually changed as the human population increased. Temperate forests attracted more and more people who saw this biome as a place where they could find shelter, food, and wood to build their fires and homes. The temperate forests of Europe were

The First Tools

The first stone tools made by humans were discovered in Africa and are more than two million years old.

the first to disappear. About one thousand years ago, nearly 80 percent of central Europe was a temperate forest biome. Today, this biome covers only about 20 percent of this region.

This man is using an axe to cut down a tree.

The Americas

While the forests in Europe were being cut down, the Indians of North America were still following their traditional methods for growing food. They cut down only a small area of forest, planted their crops, and moved on when the soil was exhausted. But with the arrival of the first European settlers more than three hundred years ago, the trees in the temperate forests of North America soon fell in much larger numbers.

Eager to bring more people to the country, the U.S. government provided land at a very reasonable price. The only

This Amish farmland in Pennsylvania was once a temperate forest biome.

requirement was that the new owner improve the land. This meant cutting down the trees on it to make way for farmland. As people began clearing the temperate forests, small communities gradually appeared. Businesses and factories soon followed. This meant even more clearing of the land.

In just one hundred years, from 1870 to 1970, much of the temperate forest in the United States was cut down. For example, about 30 percent of the land in Maine was cleared to make way for farmland. In all, more than 300 million acres (121,500,000 hectares) of temperate forest land in the United States were turned into farmland.

Insects

Humans have not been the only threat to temperate forests. Insects have also caused much damage. This is especially true when insects from elsewhere are introduced, often accidentally, into a forest biome. One of the best examples of this threat is the gypsy moth.

This tree lost its leaves because of gypsy moths (shown here in an earlier stage as caterpillars). Today, attempts to control the gypsy moth population include the use of chemicals, predators, and traps.

The gypsy moth has existed in the temperate forests of Europe and Asia for thousands of years. During part of its life cycle, the gypsy moth feeds on plants, including the leaves of temperate forest trees. Gypsy moths can eat all the leaves on a tree in just one week. Without their leaves in summer, trees are more susceptible to disease. If the trees lose their leaves for three consecutive years, they are likely to die.

The gypsy moth population in Europe and Asia has been kept under control by the moths' natural predators. As a result, gypsy moths have not been a threat to the temperate forests in these parts of the world. The story, however, is very different in the temperate forests in the United States, where gypsy moths and their predators are not native and therefore have no enemies.

In the late 1860s, a French artist named Etienne Trouvelot returned from a trip to France to his home near Boston, Massachusetts. Trouvelot had an interest in insects, searching for any that might be able to make silk like the silkworm. Trouvelot decided that gypsy moths were worth investigating and brought some of their eggs back from Europe. He apparently tried to incubate some of the eggs in a laboratory he had set up in his home. Some insects, however, escaped. Trouvelot was aware of the potential danger and informed the authorities. Nothing was done, however, to retrieve the escaped insects because other people did not share Trouvelot's concern.

In 1882, Trouvelot moved back to France. That same year, the first gypsy moth outbreak in the United States took place. Most of the trees in the area where Trouvelot had lived lost their leaves. The gypsy moths slowly spread throughout the temperate forest biome in the United States. In the early 1980s, they appeared as far south as Virginia. In just twenty years, about 4.5 million acres (1,822,500 ha) of trees in Virginia alone lost their leaves to gypsy moths. From just outside Boston, the gypsy moth has spread and today threatens the temperate forests in fifteen states.

Another threat to temperate forests is a beetle that attacks elm trees. Infected trees develop Dutch elm disease, which gets its name because it was first identified in the Netherlands in 1921. In 1930, the first case of Dutch elm disease in the United States was reported in Cleveland, Ohio. Apparently, the beetle was accidentally introduced into this country through a shipment of elm logs from Europe. Finding American elm trees to be perfect hosts, the beetle spread quickly through the temperate forest biome. In just forty years, some 77 million trees were killed by Dutch elm disease.

*American elm trees
have been killed by
Dutch elm disease.*

*This elm is dying from
the disease. Beetles
carrying the disease
bored through the
bark to the interior
of the tree.*

Threat from Above

Air pollution also poses a threat to temperate forests. Burning petroleum products, such as gasoline and oil, releases gases into the atmosphere. Some of these gases combine with moisture in the air to produce substances called **acids.** An acid is a substance that has a sour taste and can irritate the skin. The acids released into the atmosphere combine with moisture in the air. The acids then fall to Earth with rain or snow. This is called **acid precipitation.**

Over time, acid precipitation can kill trees. The precipitation soaks into the soil, where it removes **nutrients.** A nutrient is a substance that a living thing needs to survive and grow. Acid precipitation has damaged or destroyed many trees in the temperate forest.

The destruction of temperate forests, whether by humans, insects, or acid precipitation, has contributed to another problem. Gases released into the atmosphere from the burning of fuels help trap the sun's heat. This causes a slight warming of Earth's atmosphere, a process known as global warming. One of the gases responsible for global warming is carbon dioxide. Trees, like all green plants, remove carbon dioxide from the atmosphere. When there are fewer trees, however, less carbon dioxide can be removed. This will likely promote even more global warming. If this does happen, life on Earth will be affected, including the plants and animals that live in temperate forests.

Household Acids

Two common household acids are lemon juice and vinegar.

27

At certain times of the year, nature takes on many dazzling colors within the temperate forest.

Chapter Three

Plants of the Forest

Each fall, the leaves in some temperate forests put on a spectacular color display before the dried foliage drops to the ground. These forests are known as **temperate deciduous forests.** Not all temperate forests, however, have trees that lose their leaves as the cold weather of winter approaches. In fact, the trees in some temperate forests have leaves that stay green throughout the year. These forests are known as **temperate evergreen forests**. Both

Unlike evergreen trees in the temperate forests, the leaves of deciduous trees turn bright colors in the fall before they fall to the forest floor. This mountain stream is surrounded by the colors of fall.

types of temperate forests are home to a variety of plant life in addition to trees.

Temperate Evergreen Forests

Temperate evergreen forests can be found in parts of the temperate zones where the climate is cooler and drier throughout the year. The soil in these areas is usually very rocky, sandy, and poor in nutrients. This combination of cool climate, dry conditions, and sandy soil favors the growth of evergreen trees, especially pines. Other types of evergreen trees include

spruce, fir, and hemlock. All of these trees have **adaptations** that allow them to survive in cooler weather and sandy soil. An adaptation is a feature that increases a living thing's chances of survival in its environment.

One adaptation of evergreen trees that grow in cool, dry climates is their unusual leaves. Rather than being broad and flat, evergreen leaves are narrow and round. Such leaves are known as needles. Compared to typical leaves, needles have much less exposed surface area. With less surface area, needles lose less water than leaves do. As a result, needles have a better chance of survival in a dry climate.

All trees absorb the water they need from the soil through their roots. But evergreen trees grow in a sandy soil that does not retain water for very long. Another adaptation in these trees is a shallow root system. Their roots spread far and wide, but not very deep, through the soil. This enables the trees to absorb as much water as possible before the water seeps deeper into the ground and is out of reach.

Trees in temperate evergreen forests in cool climates have needlelike leaves that stay green all year.

These trees in the temperate rain forest of Washington State's Olympic Park are covered with green mosses that thrive because of moisture.

A temperate evergreen forest grows along the Pacific coastline of North America and extends from Alaska to California. In California, giant redwoods and sequoias grow to be more than 330 feet (100 meters) tall. Hemlocks, firs, and big-leafed maples also tower hundreds of feet in forests along the Pacific Coast.

Temperate evergreen forests are also in Australia, Tasmania, and New Zealand. These parts of the world receive much more rainfall than the Pacific coastline of North America. Some areas in these countries receive as much as 150 inches (381 cm) of rainfall each year.

Some of the world's tallest trees grow in these temperate evergreen forests. For example, the forest in Australia is home to the mountain ash, which can grow to be more than 330 feet (100 m) tall. The mountain ash is a type of eucalyptus tree. More than 75 percent of the trees in Australia are eucalyptus trees. The leaves of these trees secrete an oil. When sunlight strikes these oil droplets, a blue color is reflected. Because there are so many eucalyptus trees, parts of Australia are often covered in a blue haze.

Temperate Deciduous Forests

All summer long, green is the dominant color in a deciduous forest. This color comes from a green pigment called **chlorophyll.** This pigment captures light energy from the sun and uses it to make sugars in a process called **photosynthesis.** These sugars are used by all parts of the tree to survive and grow.

As the weather begins to get cooler, the chlorophyll in a leaf starts to break down. Other colors that had been hidden by the chlorophyll begin to show. These include the reds, yellows, browns, and oranges that create colorful foliage in the fall.

As the temperature drops, a layer also begins to form between the twig and base of each leaf stem. This layer acts like a pair of scissors, slowly cutting across the base of each leaf stem. When the cut is complete, a puff of wind or a few drops of rain will cause the leaf to fall to the ground. Nutrients

The American chestnut tree was once common to many temperate deciduous forests. By 1940, most of them had died from a disease that spread from foreign chestnut trees brought to New York City in 1904.

stored in the roots will keep the tree alive until the next spring, when leaf buds full of chlorophyll reappear.

Some deciduous forests are dominated by one type of tree. In areas near the midwestern United States, the forest consists almost entirely of maple trees or beech trees. Usually, however, a deciduous forest has a mixture of two kinds of trees, such as oak and hickory or maple and beech. Still other forests may contain a variety of trees, including ash, aspen, basswood, birch, black cherry, buckeye, chestnut, and magnolia.

Layers of the Temperate Forests

The leaves on the trees in a temperate forest tower over everything below. In effect, these leaves make up the top layer of life in the forest. This top layer is called the **canopy** of the forest. Beneath the canopy are several other layers, each made up of various kinds of plant life.

The canopy blocks most of the sunlight from penetrating deeper into the forest. Therefore, plants growing just beneath the upper canopy must be adapted to survive in limited sunlight. The second layer is also made of trees. Some of these trees will continue to grow tall and eventually become part of the canopy. Others will stop growing and remain in this lower layer. In some temperate forests, these shorter trees include redbuds, dogwoods, and hollies.

The trees in the second layer are adapted to survive in the limited sunlight and drier conditions created by the canopy. For example, the leaves on holly trees stay green all year. They continue to carry out photosynthesis long after the leaves of the canopy have fallen to the ground. Holly leaves are also thick and waxy, which are adaptations that enable them to conserve water.

Beneath the shorter trees is a third layer made up of shrubs. These shrubs include blueberry, huckleberry, azalea, mountain laurel, rhododendron, and one with a rather scary name— devil's club. This shrub can grow to be up to 8 feet (2.4 m) tall with leaves as big as 3 feet (90 cm) across. Its stems are thick and crooked. The large spines on the stems give this shrub its

Making Music

The wood from holly trees is used to make piano keys, which are then dyed black.

name. These spines, which are more than 2 inches (1 cm) long, can scratch anyone or anything that touches them.

Small, flowering plants form the fourth layer. These plants include larkspur, lady's slipper, foxglove, willow herb, and bluebell. Like the trees and shrubs of the forest, most of these plants produce the food they need through photosynthesis. Some plants in this layer of the forest, however, cannot make all the food they need. These plants get their additional food by taking it from other plants. An example of a plant with this adaptation is the cow wheat plant that grows in the European temperate forest. This plant gets its name because cows love to eat it, and people once believed that its seeds could be ground into wheat. The cow wheat plant attaches its roots to those of other plants and then sucks out the nutrients from their food.

Scattered among the plants of the temperate forest are mosses, ferns, and mushrooms. Unlike mosses and ferns, mushrooms are not plants. To obtain nutrients, mushrooms release chemicals that dissolve dead plants and animals. Mushrooms then take in the nutrients they need from this dissolved material.

The fifth and lowest layer in a temperate forest is the soil. In evergreen forests, this soil is poor in nutrients. Needles do fall from their branches, returning some nutrients to the soil, but not as many as the leaves from deciduous trees return. Furthermore, the needles take many years to decompose, or break down, so the soil does not get the nutrients right away.

Smelling Fresh

The bark from the stem of devil's club was once used as a deodorant.

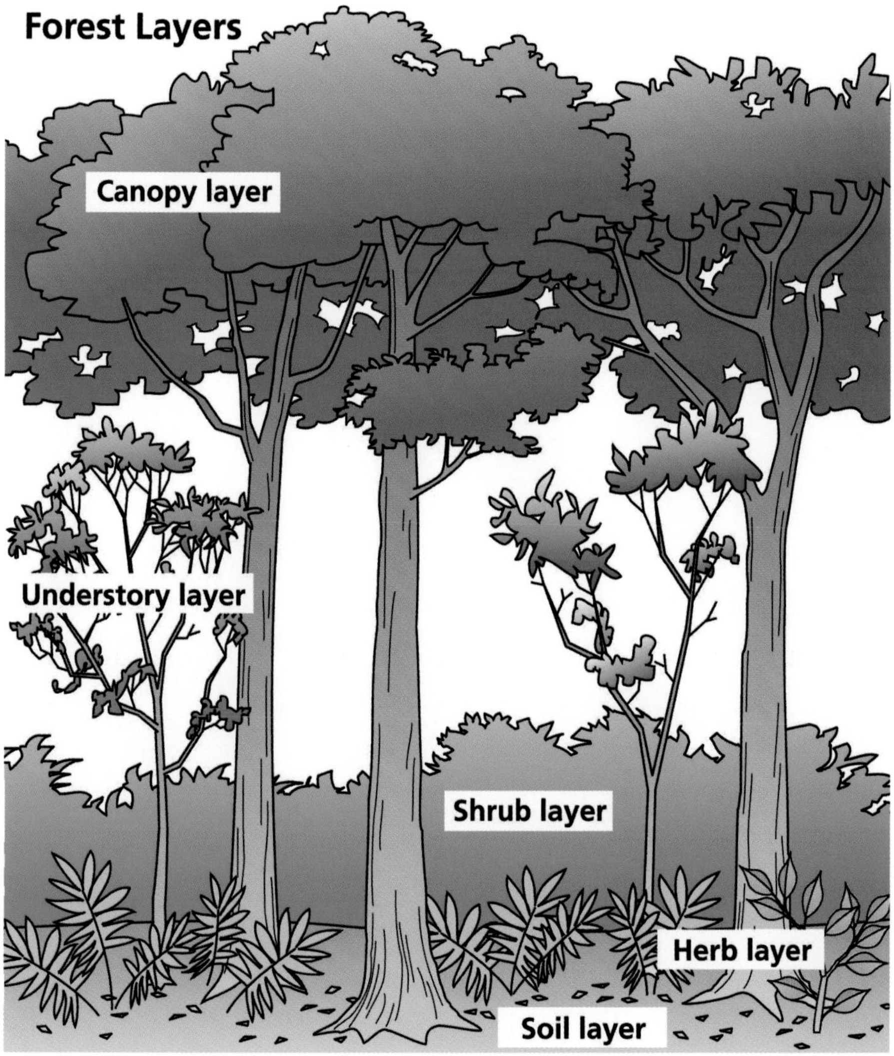

Forest Layers

Canopy layer

Understory layer

Shrub layer

Herb layer

Soil layer

A temperate forest can be divided into five layers, as shown here.

In contrast, the leaves that fall every year in deciduous forests, especially those that contain maple trees, decompose within a year or two. The nutrients that are released enrich the soil, supporting a greater variety of **organisms,** or living things, than are found in an evergreen forest. These organisms include an interesting assortment of animals.

Bamboo makes up 99 percent of a panda's diet.

Chapter Four

Animals of the Forest

Like the plants in a temperate forest, animals that live in this biome are also adapted to it. Pandas are an example of these animals. Pandas live in the temperate forests of China and Tibet, where they feed almost exclusively on bamboo, eating its leaves, stems, and shoots.

Pandas have several adaptations for eating bamboo, which is tough and stringy. A bone on their wrist is so large that it acts like a thumb, enabling pandas to grasp the bamboo with their paws.

Their teeth are large and flat, providing a surface for them to grind the tough bamboo before swallowing it. Their digestive system has a thick lining that prevents woody splinters from doing any damage to their organs.

Despite these adaptations, pandas can digest only about 20 percent of the bamboo they eat. In comparison, cows digest about 60 percent of the grass they eat. As a result, pandas must eat continuously to get the nutrients they need. Pandas spend between twelve and sixteen hours per day eating. They eat between 20 and 40 pounds (9 and 18 kilograms) of bamboo every day. If tender young shoots are not available, a panda may have to eat as much as 80 pounds (36 kg) of stems and leaves per day to survive. Pandas are just one example of temperate forest animals that depend on plants to survive.

Diet Preferences

Animals that eat plants, such as pandas, are known as **herbivores.** Not all herbivores are as large as pandas. In fact, some are quite small. These herbivores include many insects and birds. One plant may provide enough food to feed thousands of herbivores.

An example of such a plant is the oak tree. One oak tree can produce ninety thousand acorns per year. All these acorns can feed a lot of squirrels, woodpeckers, and deer that live in the forest. In addition, the sap, buds, and leaves of one oak tree may support more than one thousand different types of insects.

Some forest animals, known as **carnivores,** eat other animals. Examples include foxes and owls, which prey on mice. Hawks swoop down from the sky to snare smaller birds, which may be searching for seeds or earthworms on the ground. Tree frogs, which are less than 1 inch (2.54 cm) long, capture mosquitoes, spiders, crickets, and anything else they can fit into their mouths. Moles burrow underground, searching for worms and beetles.

Animals that eat both plants and animals are known as **omnivores.** A forest omnivore with one of the largest appetites is the black bear. These animals once lived throughout North America, including biomes other than temperate forests. Hunters, however, drove many of them to forests. About thirty thousand black bears are killed by hunters each year.

A black bear can weigh as much as 500 pounds (227 kg) and can stand 6 feet (1.8 m) tall.

Contrary to popular belief, black bears rarely attack humans. But if these bears are provoked or suddenly surprised (as they sometimes are by humans), they can become dangerous. Black bears are mainly herbivores, eating berries, fruits, and acorns. In leaner times, the bears may eat insects and any small mice they are able to catch. Like pandas, black bears spend most of the day eating.

Feeding Relationships

Organisms other than plants depend on each other for food. These dependencies are known as feeding relationships. Feeding relationships are often much more complex than they may appear.

Pandas are an exception in that they live almost exclusively on bamboo. This is an example of a feeding relationship known as a **food chain.** This food chain has two links: a panda bear and bamboo grass. Food chains often consist of three or more links. An example is a hawk that eats a bird that has eaten a caterpillar that has fed on leaves. How many links does this food chain have?

Food chains, however, do not exist in isolation. Rather, they are linked with one another to form more complex feeding relationships known as **food webs.** The foundation of every food web on land consists of plants, which are known as **producers,** because they produce the foods that all life depends on. Animals are known as **consumers** because they cannot produce their own food. They must instead consume it. A caterpillar that eats the leaves of a maple tree in a temperate forest is known as a primary, or first-level, consumer. The American redstart bird that eats the caterpillar is a secondary, or second-level, consumer. The broad-winged hawk that eats the redstart is a tertiary, or third-level, consumer.

The redstart is not the only type of bird hawks eat. And in addition to birds, hawks eat chipmunks, shrews, voles, lizards, frogs, caterpillars, and earthworms. All these organisms are parts of various food chains. The hawk is just one organism that links all these food chains into a giant food web.

A Temperate Forest Food Web

Carnivores — Fox, Weasel, Hawk

Snake, Frog

Herbivores — Rabbit, Mouse, Sparrow, Grasshopper

Primary Producers — Plants

The arrows show how energy in the form of food moves through a food web. The arrows point from the organism to its consumer.

Survival Techniques

Animals living in a temperate forest display a variety of survival techniques. Many animals simply hide during the day and venture out only at night to search for a meal. Some live in burrows for protection. These include animals with such interesting names as raccoon dogs, ant lions, and deer mice. Raccoon dogs, which are native to Asian temperate forests, are

Tiny but Deadly

Clinging to the skin of a deer mouse can be a very tiny organism known as a deer tick. In summer, a deer tick obtains nutrients by sucking a drop or two of the mouse's blood. This blood provides enough nutrients for the tick to survive through the fall and winter. In spring, however, the tick needs another blood meal. This time its target is a deer. These ticks, which are often infected with bacteria, can crawl from deer onto humans who wander through a temperate forest.

Humans may also accidentally get a tick from their pets. Once a tick attaches itself to a human, it will again seek a blood meal. While it feeds, the tick may infect the human with bacteria that can cause Lyme disease, Rocky Mountain spotted fever, and other serious diseases. Some of these diseases can be fatal if not treated.

dogs that look like raccoons. These animals will eat anything they can find. An ant lion is an insect that devours ants by grasping them in its jaws and then sucking their blood. Deer mice are part of many food webs in which they are eaten by a variety of carnivores, including snakes and owls.

Some animals that cannot hide from danger survive by blending in with their surroundings. This is known as camouflage. This adaptation for survival, however, does not always work well in a temperate forest, because the colors change with the seasons. For example, a brown-colored deer may be well camouflaged in summer and fall, but it becomes a clearly visible target in winter, when there is little foliage.

Another adaptation involves two different kinds of organisms. One organism has evolved, or slowly changed over time, so that it looks like another organism. This adaptation is known as **mimicry.** A well-known example involves two kinds of butterflies. One is the monarch butterfly, which is distasteful to birds. Once a bird has eaten a monarch, it is not likely to pick up one again. In contrast, viceroy butterflies would make a tasty meal for birds. But birds are not likely to eat viceroys because viceroys have evolved over many thousands of years to look like monarchs.

Birds leave monarch butterflies alone because they don't taste good. The viceroy butterfly on the left has a better chance of survival because it mimics the monarch butterfly on the right.

Two Choices

When winter arrives, many of the animals in a temperate forest must make a choice. They can stay and face the freezing temperatures or leave the area for a warmer climate. Snow makes food more difficult to find. Many animals, such as deer and mice, spend almost all their waking time in winter searching for food. Deer may have to settle for twigs and bark, while mice must scramble to find seeds and nuts buried in the snow.

Some animals, however, do not search for food at all. Rather, they spend their winters in **hibernation.** Animals that hibernate include the black bear and the woodchuck, which is also known as the groundhog. During hibernation, all body processes, including respiration and digestion, slow down. For example, a woodchuck's heartbeat slows down from more than one hundred beats per minute to as few as fifteen. Its body temperature drops from about 95 degrees Fahrenheit (35 degrees Celsius) to about 45° F (7° C). A woodchuck's hibernation starts in October and lasts until March or April, depending on when the weather gets warm enough for it to emerge from its underground burrow.

Woodchucks are herbivores that eat grasses, leaves, and herbs. They also eat farm crops, including alfalfa and corn.

During the summer and fall, a black bear gains as much as a 6-inch (15-cm) layer of fat around its body. When winter arrives and food is scarce, this fat will provide the energy the black bear needs to stay alive while it hibernates for the winter. Most black bears, however, will periodically arouse from their hibernation during the winter and roam the forest, especially on warmer days.

Not all animals, however, have the adaptations to survive the winter in a temperate forest. These animals must leave, or migrate, to warmer climates. Some travel great distances. Monarch butterflies, for example, fly from temperate forests near the Great Lakes all the way to Mexico, a distance of more than 2,000 miles (3,219 km). In spring, they begin their return flight.

Winter is not the only time animals leave the forest in large numbers. Sometimes they do it in the summer when a fire is raging through a temperate forest.

Most people think fires destroy forests. A fire, however, can actually be helpful in the long-term maintenance of a temperate forest.

Chapter Five

Forest Fires

In summer, frequent rainfall usually keeps the temperate forest moist enough to prevent fires. During a drought, however, all the dry brush in a forest acts as fuel that can be easily ignited. In some cases, lightning may be the cause of a fire. In others, humans may be responsible, perhaps by carelessly tossing a match into the woods or by not putting out a campfire.

At one time, every effort was made to put out a forest fire as soon as it was spotted. Today, however, fires are started deliberately by forestry officials. These fires are allowed to burn under controlled conditions and under the careful

Fire Extinguishers

Though forest fires can be helpful to forests, forest rangers still make every effort to extinguish those that are accidentally started by people.

supervision of trained forest rangers. A major goal of these controlled fires is to reduce the amount of brush and dead wood that accumulate over the years. As a result, a wildfire that can quickly get out of control is less likely to start. Controlled fires are started for another reason. These fires help to maintain the temperate forest.

How Fires Help the Forest

Fires are more likely to start in forests when the climate gets hot and dry in summer. Temperate evergreen forests in the western and southern United States are most at risk. Fortunately, trees in these forests are adapted to survive fires. Their bark, for example, is very thick and acts as insulation so that the entire tree does not burn. In addition, their cones protect the seeds inside from burning.

In some types of evergreen trees, the seeds remain inside the cones until the cones are opened by the heat from a fire. If there were no fire, the seeds would not be released, and new trees would not replace those that died or were destroyed. Fires also release the nutrients stored in pine needles that otherwise would take years to decompose on the ground. These burned pine needles enrich the soil. The seeds of some plants also do not sprout unless they are exposed to the heat from a fire.

Fires can help maintain a temperate forest only if they occur occasionally. If they happen frequently, the damage they do will outweigh any benefits they provide. In 1988, the summer was extremely hot and dry in Yellowstone National Park.

Lightning set off many fires that spread throughout the park. By the time the fires were brought under control, more than half the park was damaged. Fortunately, a forest can make a comeback even after such a devastating series of fires.

Succession

You read that glaciers once covered some of the lands where temperate forests now grow. When the glaciers retreated, all that was left behind was barren ground littered with boulders and rocks. After a raging fire, the ground can also look barren except for the stumps of dead trees. How can a forest possibly reappear on the barren land left by glaciers or a fire? The answer is through a process called **succession.**

Pitch pine forests are found in the northeastern United States. Their cones may remain closed for as long as ten years unless there is a fire to open them.

Succession is a natural process by which one community of organisms slowly replaces another community until a final stage, known as a climax community, is reached. It can take hundreds or even thousands of years for the climax community to become established. In some areas, the climax community is a temperate forest.

Lichens are called pioneer organisms because they are among the first living things to appear when succession starts.

From Lake to Forest

Succession can also change a lake into a temperate forest.

Succession begins with simple organisms known as lichens. Lichens are actually two different organisms, known as algae and fungi, that live together. The algae carry out photosynthesis and provide the pair with food. The fungi provide the pair with shelter. As a result, each organism benefits from the other. This is a relationship known as **mutualism.**

As they grow, lichens secrete substances that break off tiny pieces of rock. These pieces accumulate on the ground, where they continue to get smaller and smaller. After lichens die, they fall to the ground and decompose. The tiny pieces of rock and decaying lichens help make soil. Small plants known as mosses start to grow in the soil, which continues to build up. The soil can then support the growth of grasses and still other small plants. As these organisms die and decompose, they enrich the soil even more.

Over time, the soil becomes thick and rich enough to support trees that sprout from seeds blown into the area by the wind or carried by animals. Pine and birch trees are among the first to appear. These trees provide shade that favors the growth of maple, oak, and beech trees. What was once barren land is now a temperate forest.

Succession can slowly change barren land covered with rocks into a lush grassland.

Lost Forever

Succession does not always restore a forest biome that has been destroyed. In some cases, the destruction of a forest, whether by natural or human causes, is irreversible. An example can be seen in the villages, towns, and cities built on lands that were once temperate forests. More people live on lands that once were temperate forests than on the lands of any other biome.

Nature reserves have been set up in many temperate forests to preserve the plants and animals that live there.

Trees are not all that are lost forever when a temperate forest is destroyed. Some animals may be lost too. The destruction of temperate forests in the United States has contributed to the extinction, or permanent loss, of the Carolina parakeet, the ivory-billed woodpecker, the eastern wood buffalo, and the eastern elk. Even the number of pandas has declined as bamboo forests in China and Tibet are cut down. Hopefully, these animals and other endangered organisms living in temperate forests will not become extinct.

Glossary

acid—a substance that has a sour taste and irritates the skin

acid precipitation—moisture that contains acids and falls to Earth as rain, snow, or some other type of precipitation

adaptation—a feature that increases an organism's chances of survival

biome—a geographic area in which specific kinds of plants and animals live

canopy—the top layer in a forest that is formed by the leaves of the taller trees

carnivore—an animal that eats other animals

chlorophyll—a green pigment found in plants

consumer—an organism that depends on another organism for its food

food chain—a single pathway through which energy is passed from one organism to the next

food web—a collection of food chains that are linked to one another

herbivore—an animal that depends on plants for food

hibernation—the state in which many body processes, such as breathing, slow down

mimicry—the resemblance in appearance or behavior between two different animals

mutualism—a relationship between two different organisms in which both benefit

Northern Hemisphere—the half of Earth that is north of the equator

nutrient—a substance that an organism needs to survive and grow

omnivore—an animal that eats both plants and animals

organism—a living thing

photosynthesis—the process by which plants make sugars and other nutrients

producer—a organism that produces its own food

Southern Hemisphere—the half of Earth that is south of the equator

succession—the natural process in which one community of organisms is replaced by another community until a stable climax community is established

temperate deciduous forest—a temperate-zone forest in which the trees lose their leaves each winter

temperate evergreen forest—a temperate-zone forest in which the trees keep their needles in winter

temperate forest—a biome in which the climate of the temperate zone favors the growth of trees

To Find Out More

Books

Baldwin, Carol. *Living in a Temperate Deciduous Forest.* Chicago: Heinemann Library, 2003.

Johansson, Philip. *The Temperate Forest: A Web of Life.* Berkeley Heights, N.J.: Enslow Publishers, 2004.

Kaplan, Elizabeth. *Temperate Forest.* Tarrytown, N.Y.: Benchmark Books, 1996.

Wilkins, Sally. *Temperate Forests.* Mankato, Minn.: Bridgestone Books, 2001.

Woodward, John. *Temperate Forests.* Austin, Tex.: Raintree Steck-Vaughn, 2002.

Organizations and Online Sites

Forest Links
http://www.omsi.edu/visit/life/forestpuzzles/links.html
Learn more about how humans have affected this biome and how NASA is trying to protect temperate forests.

South American Temperate Forests
http://web.greenpeace.org/campaigns/intro?campaign_id=4011
The temperate forests of Chile and Argentina represent the largest undisturbed area of temperate forest in the world. Learn more about the organisms that live in these forests.

Temperate Forest Foundation
http://www.forestinfo.org/index.htm
Click on "Discover" to learn more about North American temperate forests, including some "Cool Facts."

U.S. Department of Agriculture Forest Service
1400 Independence Avenue, SW
Washington, DC 20250-0003
(202) 205-8333
http://www.fs.fed.us
On this site, you can search for information about a particular forest either by state or by name. You can also click on the "Just for Kids" and "Photo Video Gallery" links.

A Note on Sources

Personal experiences provided me with an excellent starting point for writing this book. My wife and I live "in the woods," surrounded by a mixed deciduous forest of white pines, pitch pines, and oaks. Nearly everything we have put into the ground has been devoured by deer, herbivores whose diet can include anything that grows in a temperate forest.

We have also witnessed the impact of a devastating fire that destroyed thousands of acres of dwarf pine trees not far from our home. Fortunately, succession started soon after. We have also witnessed what gypsy moths can do to a temperate forest. One summer, most of the trees surrounding our home lost their leaves.

To go beyond personal experience, I searched the Internet. I also referred to various governmental agencies, wildlife organizations, and educational institutions for the most reliable information.

— *Salvatore Tocci*

Index

Numbers in *italics* indicate illustrations.

acid precipitation, 27
adaptations, 31, 35, 36, 39,
    40, 44, 45, 47
Africa, 20
air pollution, 27
American Indians, *22*
American redstart bird, 43
Andes Mountains, 13–14
animals, 11, *17, 22,* 27, *38,*
    39–47, *41, 46*
Antarctic Circle, 12
Antarctica, 12
Appalachian Trail, *6,* 7–9,
    10–11, 11
Arctic Circle, 12
Argentina, 12, 13–14
Asia, 16
Australia, 14, 15, 32, 33
bamboo, *38,* 39–40, 42

Belarus, 17
Bialowieza Forest, 17, *17*
biomes, 11, 14
black bears, 41–42, *41,* 46,
    47

camouflage, 44
Canada, 12, 14
canopy, 35, *37*
carbon dioxide, 27
carnivores, 41, 44
Chile, 14
China, 16–17, 23, 39, 54
chlorophyll, 33
climax communities, 51
consumers, 42–43

deciduous forests, *28,* 29–30,
    33–34

deciduous trees, 29, 30
decomposition, 36, 37
deer, 40, 44, 46
deer mice, 43, 44
deer ticks, 44
Denmark, 17
devil's club shrubs, 35–36
Dutch elm disease, 25, *26*

equator, 12
Europe, 17, 20–21, 22, 24,
    25, 36
evergreen forests, 29–30,
    30–33, *31*, 37, 50
evergreen trees, 30–31, *31*
evolution, 45

feeding relationships, 42
food chain, 42
food webs, 42, *43*, 44
forest fires, 47, *48*, 49–51
fungi, 52
glaciers, 19–20
gypsy moths, 23–24, *24*

hemlock trees, 31, 32
herbivores, 40, 42

ice ages, 19

insects, 23–25, *24*, 27, 40,
    41, 42, 45, *45*
ivory-billed woodpeckers, 54

Japan, 16

Korea, 16

latitude, 12
lichens, 52, *52*
Lyme disease, 44

map, *13*
maple trees, 34, 37, 43
Mexico, 12, 47
mimicry, 45
monarch butterflies, 45, *45*,
    47
mosses, *32*, 36
mutualism, 52
nature reserves, *54*

New Zealand, 14, 15, *15*, 32
North America, 12, 22–23,
    32, 41
Northern Hemisphere, 12,
    13
Northern temperate zone,
    14, 16–17

nutrients, 27, 33–34, 36

omnivores, 41

Pacific Ocean, 13, 14
pandas, *38*, 39–40, 42, 54
people, 7–9, *16*, 20, *21*,
    22–23, 24–25, 40, 42,
    44, 49, 50, 53
photosynthesis, 33, 35, 36,
    52
pioneer organisms, *52*
plants, 11, *24*, 27, 29–37,
    32, *37*, *38*, 39–40, 42,
    43, *46*, 52–53, *52*
Poland, 17
Portugal, *16*, 17
primary consumers, 43
producers, 42

rainfall, 11, 14, 27, 32, 49
Russia, 17

secondary consumers, 43
Shenandoah National Park,
    10–11
soil, 30, 31, 36, *37*
Southern Hemisphere, 12,
    13

Southern temperate zone,
    13–14
succession, 51–53, *53*
sunlight, 11, 33, 35

Tasmania, 14, 15, *15*, 32
temperate deciduous forests,
    28, 29–30, *30*, 33–34
temperate evergreen forests,
    29–30, 30–33, *31*, 37,
    50
temperatures, 12, 33, 46
tertiary consumers, 43
Tibet, 23, 39, 54
Tropic of Cancer, 12
Tropic of Capricorn, 12

understory, *37*
United States, 14, 16, 19,
    20, 23, 24, 25, 34, 50,
    51, 54
Uruguay, 13, 14

Virginia, *10–11*, 25

Yellowstone National Park,
    50–51

About the Author

Salvatore Tocci taught high school and college science for almost thirty years. He has a bachelor's degree from Cornell University and a master's degree from The City University of New York.

He has written books that deal with a range of science topics, from biographies of famous scientists to a high school chemistry textbook. He has also traveled throughout the United States to present workshops at national science conventions to show teachers how to emphasize the applications of scientific knowledge to students' everyday lives.

Tocci lives in East Hampton, New York, with his wife, Patti. While having the land cleared for their house, they made sure that as few trees as possible were cut down.